Gardens Change

By Karen Baicker

W9-BIC-835

Scott Foresman
is an imprint of

Glenview, Illinois • Boston, Massachusetts • Chandler, Arizona •
Upper Saddle River, New Jersey

Photographs

Every effort has been made to secure permission and provide appropriate credit for photographic material. The publisher deeply regrets any omission and pledges to correct errors called to its attention in subsequent editions.

Unless otherwise acknowledged, all photographs are the property of Pearson Education, Inc.

Photo locators denoted as follows: Top (T), Center (C), Bottom (B), Left (L), Right (R), Background (Bkgd)

Opener: Tetra Images/Alamy
1 ©blickwinkel/Alamy Images
3 ©Peter Gerdehag/Jupiter Images
4 Getty Images
5 ©Edd Westmacott/Alamy
6 ©blickwinkel/Alamy Images
7 ©Tetra Images/Jupiter Images
8 ©Ariel Skelley/Getty Image

ISBN 13: 978-0-328-46289-6
ISBN 10:   0-328-46289-6

10 V010 14

The garden has snow.

The garden has seeds.

The garden has leaves.

The garden has flowers.

The garden has pumpkins.

The garden has kids!